(When) Did It Happen?

New Contexts for Old Testament History

John Bimson

Lecturer in Old Testament, Trinity College, Bristol

GROVE BOOKS LIMITED
RIDLEY HALL RD CAMBRIDGE CB3 9HU

Contents

The Cover Illustration is by Peter Ashton

First Impression September 2003
ISSN 1365-490X
ISBN 1 85174 541 6

Introduction

1

In his recent book The Lost Testament *(London: Century, 2002), David Rohl returns to a theory he first launched in a popular form in 1995.*

Rohl has some highly unorthodox ideas about Egyptian chronology, and these enable him to offer new and surprising links between Egypt and the Old Testament. By placing OT events in a fresh context, Rohl seems to provide striking confirmation of the OT's historical reliability.

Rohl had published aspects of his radical theory as long ago as the late 1980s, but it was first widely publicized in his lavishly illustrated book *A Test of Time: The Bible—from Myth to History* (London: Century, 1995). This was accompanied by a three-part TV series, *Pharaohs and Kings: A Biblical Quest,* shown on Channel 5. Rohl stated explicitly in that book that he hoped it would 'bring the issue of the historicity of the Old Testament back into the spotlight' (p 367).

By placing OT events in a fresh context, Rohl seems to provide striking confirmation of the OT's historical reliability

It is clear from my postbag over the last few years that Rohl has many Christian readers who want to know how plausible his ideas are. For some of these enquirers, the historical reliability of the OT evidently matters a great deal. For others, that is less of an issue. But they are still intrigued; they want to know whether the standard histories of the ancient Near East could really be so wrong.

In this booklet I will try to address both kinds of question. I will look at how far the OT's historical reliability matters, and (if so) whether Rohl's radical theory is its best defence. But I am also writing from a belief that the truth is important for its own sake—that if the history books have got it wrong, the record needs putting straight!

For those not familiar with Rohl's ideas, I will begin with a brief outline of the theory set out in *A Test of Time* (hereafter *TT*).

2   Changing Centuries

Rohl argues that we have miscalculated Egyptian chronology. He believes that a number of pharaohs ruled in parallel in the 'Third Intermediate Period', rather than one after the other, so that the period known as the New Kingdom (18th to 20th Dynasties) moves closer to the present by almost 350 years—see the table on page 10. The results for biblical history are dramatic.

In what Rohl calls the New Chronology, the great warrior-pharaoh Ramesses II moves down from his conventional date of 1279–1213 BC to 943–877 BC.[1] Ramesses leaves his familiar role as chief candidate for the pharaoh of the Exodus, and becomes instead 'King Shishak of Egypt,' who invaded Judah after the death of Solomon (1 Kings 14.25). The pharaoh whose daughter Solomon married (1 Kings 9.16) is identified as Haremheb, successor-but-one to Tutankhamun, and last ruler of the 18th Dynasty.

Two reigns before Tutankhamun, Egypt was ruled by the quasi-monotheist Akhenaten (conventionally 1353–1337 BC). The New Chronology makes him contemporary with Saul and David in the late 11th century BC. In 1887 at El-Amarna, the site of Akhenaten's royal court, a large number of inscribed clay tablets were found. These turned out to be diplomatic correspondence from Assyria, Babylonia, the Hittites and the kinglets of Syria-Palestine— the famous Amarna Letters. In the New Chronology they no longer throw light on the politics of the 14th century BC, but instead illuminate the rise of Israel's monarchy.

Rohl produces an impressive list of parallels between the political situation reflected in the Letters and that of Saul's time. But he goes further and suggests that we can identify King Saul himself among the Amarna correspondents. Saul is known from the tablets as Labaya, and his son Ishbaal (Ishbosheth) also wrote to Egypt as Mutbaal. In one of Mutbaal's letters to pharaoh, Rohl finds references to David, Jesse, Joab and Baanah. The Habiru, whose marauding activities are complained of by other Amarna correspondents, are the Hebrew warriors of Saul and David.

The Exodus Revisited

Rohl's New Chronology also allows him to take a fresh look at the vexed question of the date of the Exodus. The OT is notoriously unclear about when the Exodus happened. It not only fails to name any of the pharaohs mentioned in Genesis and Exodus, but even provides conflicting clues.

According to 1 Kings 6.1, the Exodus took place 480 years before the founding of the Temple in the 4th year of Solomon. Taken at face value, this dates the Exodus around 1450/1440 BC. However, most scholars place greater weight on Exodus 1.11, which says that the enslaved Israelites built Pithom and Raamses for the pharaoh. The name Raamses recalls the Egyptian city of Pi-Ramesse, built in the Nile Delta under Ramesses II. This is one reason why Ramesses II has often been identified as the pharaoh of the Exodus and/or the oppression. In terms of the conventional chronology, Exodus 1.11 therefore seems to favour a date in the 13th century BC for the Exodus.

In the New Chronology, however, Ramesses II is out of the running as pharaoh of the Exodus, and Rohl adopts the 15th century BC date indicated by 1 Kings 6.1. Combining this with his shorter chronology, he is able to synchronize the Exodus with the collapse of Egyptian power at the end of the 13th Dynasty. The pharaoh under whom Moses grew up is identified as Sobekhotep IV, the last powerful pharaoh of that dynasty, with the Exodus occurring under an obscure king called Dudumose.

At the site of Tell el-Dab'a in the Nile Delta, archaeologists have found plentiful evidence of settlement by groups from Canaan during the 13th Dynasty. One stratum at the site (labelled Stratum G) ended with some kind of calamity which led to bodies being buried without ceremony in shallow pits. After this catastrophe the site was abandoned for a while. In Rohl's theory, the settlers from Canaan were the Israelites, the high death-toll was caused by the tenth plague, and the abandonment of the site is due to the Exodus.

Joseph

When we move back in time to the preceding 12th Dynasty, evidence for Joseph comes to light. Rohl dates his arrival in Egypt and his elevation to the office of Vizier to the reign of Senuseret (or Sesostris) III. The years of plenty and of famine are identified with the aid of texts that record the level of the Nile.

Rohl's final revelation is an empty tomb, associated with the remains of a smashed statue of a foreign dignitary. The tomb is identified as that of Joseph, and Rohl gives us a beautiful reconstruction of the statue, which he believes is a portrait of Joseph as Vizier.

Rohl's Approach to the OT

Rohl argues his case persuasively and his proposed links between Egypt and the OT are seductive. But is it really possible to shorten Egyptian history by 350 years? I will address that question in Chapter 3. Here I want to look briefly at Rohl's approach to the OT.

Rohl begins both *TT* and *The Lost Testament* by quoting scholars who are deeply sceptical of the OT's historicity. This scepticism is probably the consensus today. According to archaeologist Israel Finkelstein, 90% of scholars do not believe there was ever an Exodus from Egypt, 80% do not think there was a conquest of Canaan as described in the book of Joshua, and around 50% do not think there was a powerful united monarchy.[2] It is clear that Rohl sees his New Chronology as an antidote to the prevailing scepticism. Is he pandering to readers who need evidence for the Bible's historical reliability in order to feel secure in their faith? In an interview with The Learning Channel, Rohl acknowledged that his defence of the OT's historicity 'is of great comfort to people of faith who have long been fed up with being told that the Bible is a fairy tale.'[3]

On the other hand, Rohl is open about the fact that he does not write from a faith position.[4] 'I have no religious axe to grind—I am simply an historian in search of some historical truth' (*TT*, p 11). Anyone reading *The Lost Testament* will soon find that his approach to the early chapters of Genesis is a long way from that of a Christian fundamentalist. He is also at pains to stress that his reasons for questioning the conventional chronology sprang from his Egyptological studies, and not from any wish to support the historicity of the OT (*TT*, p 11).

So what is Rohl's attitude to the OT? 'In my view the biblical text—just like any other ancient document—should be treated as a *potentially* reliable historical source until it can be demonstrated to be otherwise' (*Lost Testament*, p 3). For him, the historicity of the OT was an outcome, not a presupposition, of his research: 'Without initially starting out to discover the historical Bible, I have come to the conclusion that much of the Old Testament contains real history' (*TT*, p 367).

But, of course, this confirmation of the OT's historicity depends on his application of the New Chronology. Would he have arrived at this conclusion without the New Chronology? The implication is that he would have become part of the sceptical consensus. We are left with a number of related questions which will occupy us in the following chapters:

1   Is Rohl's New Chronology viable?

2   If we believe that the OT's historical reliability matters, but decide that Rohl's New Chronology is not viable, what are we left with?

3   If we believe that the OT's reliability does *not* matter, does the debate over chronology have any relevance to OT studies?

Criticisms of the New Chronology 3

Rohl's revision has had a frosty reception from the scholarly community—from both defenders and detractors of the OT's historicity.[5]

But he has some supporters, and is also an able defender of his own ideas. As a result some robust debate can be found in the pages of the *Journal of the Ancient Chronology Forum* and online.[6] Space forbids more than a few comments here. Instead of examining Rohl's specific identifications of biblical events and characters with others known from Egyptian sources, I will concentrate on problems with the larger picture.

In what follows I will be using the terms Middle Bronze Age, Late Bronze Age and Iron Age. These are potentially misleading for the layperson, so a few words of explanation are needed. These terms have nothing to do with the use of different metals in the ancient world. They are the archaeologist's labels for periods characterized by different pottery styles. Hence, when an archaeologist says a particular stratum belongs to the Late Bronze II period, she means that it contains pottery types that have come to be classified as belonging to the second subdivision of the Late Bronze Age. In the absence of other criteria, pottery styles provide the main yardstick for dates in ancient Palestine.

Exodus and Conquest

One of the most serious problems in biblical archaeology has been a lack of evidence for the Israelite Conquest of Canaan. In 1978 I attempted to solve this by identifying the Conquest with the collapse of some of Canaan's major cities at the end of the Middle Bronze Age.[7] This event is normally dated to mid-16th century BC, but I argued for redating it by over a hundred years, to the late 15th century BC. In this way I sought to relate the destructions to the early date for the Exodus (that is, *c* 1450 BC, based on 1 Kings 6.1).

Rohl's treatment of the Conquest is superficially similar, and he cites what I have written about Jericho at some length in support of his own conclusions (*TT*, pp 305–308). However, there are some important differences, and I find weaknesses in Rohl's argument.

Rohl follows me in identifying the Israelites as the destroyers of Middle Bronze Age Jericho (a large, fortified city which came to a fiery end). However, he departs from me in the way he dates that event within the Middle Bronze Age. As we saw in Chapter 2, Rohl thinks he has found evidence of the 10th plague and the Exodus in Stratum G at Tell el-Dab'a. In terms of Palestine's archaeological periods, this event lines up with the end of a subdivision of the Middle Bronze Age known as MB IIA. This synchronism forces Rohl to put the fall of Jericho (and other cities mentioned in the Conquest narratives) in the following subdivision, called MB IIB.

This is simply much too early in the Middle Bronze Age to square with the pottery evidence. That evidence makes it clear that Jericho was destroyed *at the very end* of the Middle Bronze Age (at the end of the subdivision known as MB IIC). Rohl places the Conquest about 150 years earlier than the evidence will allow. In short, Rohl's identification of the Exodus with the calamity at the end of Stratum G at Tell el-Dab'a leaves us with no viable setting for the Conquest. Without one, it remains unconvincing.

The Problem of Samaria

Rohl's overall scheme comes up against a difficulty at Samaria. According to 1 Kings 16.24, the city of Samaria was founded in the reign of Omri (c 885–873 BC). If Rohl is right, its earliest phase should be represented by Late Bronze Age pottery, since the Late Bronze Age ends later than this in his revision (c 820 BC according to *TT*, p 175). But no Late Bronze Age pottery has turned up at Samaria. Instead, Samaria's earliest Israelite pottery belongs to the first phase of the Iron Age (which followed the Late Bronze Age). In other words, the Late Bronze Age ends too late in Rohl's scheme.[8]

350 Years is Too Many

The problem at Samaria is one of many that seem to rule out a 350-year reduction. For example, we have a good deal of genealogical data which spans Egypt's Third Intermediate Period, and to accommodate this within his scheme, Rohl has to assume an average generation length of only 20 years. This is almost certainly too short and no contemporary evidence supports it.[9]

But without his 350-year reduction of the New Kingdom, Rohl's most seductive identifications for the early monarchy will not work. The Amarna Letters cannot refer to events in the time of Saul, Ramesses II cannot have been the biblical Shishak, and so on. If David Rohl's New Chronology is wrong, does that mean that no major revision of ancient Near Eastern chronology is possible?

Shaking the Pillars 4

David Rohl's New Chronology is probably the best-known attempt to rewrite the history of the ancient world.

But he is not alone in questioning the accepted reconstruction. Several pairs of hands are currently braced against the pillars of conventional chronology, and if any of them manages to bring down what one archaeologist calls 'the whole ramshackle chronological structure,'[10] then the setting and historicity of the OT will face a major reassessment.

Centuries of Darkness

A book which preceded Rohl's *TT*, and which he acknowledges 'exposed the flaws in the conventional chronology of the Old World' (*Lost Testament*, p 3), was *Centuries of Darkness*, written by ancient historian Peter James and four colleagues.[11] *Centuries of Darkness* (hereafter *CD*) provides an impressive survey of strange gaps and anomalies which characterize the conventional chronology. The area under review is not just the ancient Near East but the entire Mediterranean world as far west as Spain, with forays southwards into Nubia and northwards into central Europe.

The book catalogues numerous unresolved disputes in which authorities have differed by as much as 250 years over the dating of a particular archaeological stratum (occupation level) or ancient culture. In some areas (for example Anatolia, Greece, Nubia), conventional dating requires the insertion of a 'dark age' between periods which, by all other criteria, would seem to have followed each other without a break. All this evidence points to the conclusion that the date currently given to the end of the Late Bronze Age, roughly 1200 BC, is about 250 years too early. Anomalies would be resolved and gaps closed if it could end around 950 BC instead.

Egypt as the Problem

Seeking the 'culprit' behind this widespread problem, James and his colleagues follow the trail to Egypt. In every case the troublesome dates have

Several pairs of hands are currently braced against the pillars of conventional chronology

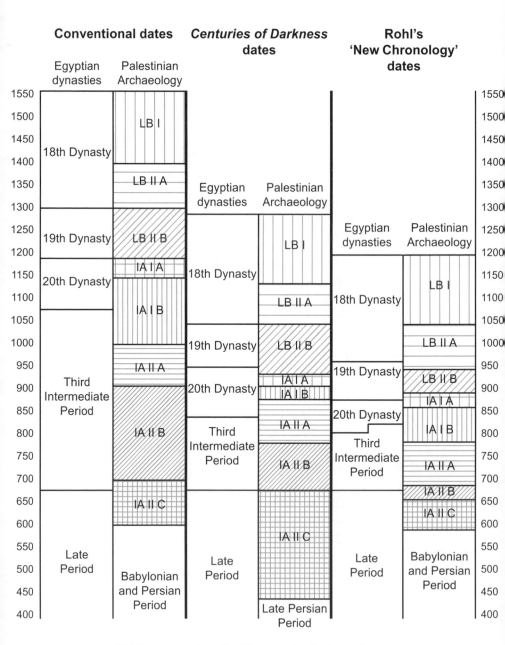

Table comparing the three main dating schemes

been derived, directly or indirectly, from the current Egyptian chronology. In fact there are problems within Egyptian chronology itself that suggest something is seriously at fault there.

The authors highlight a number of anomalies in what is known as Egypt's Third Intermediate Period (conventionally *c* 1070–664 BC). In their view, these anomalies are evidence that the Third Intermediate Period should really be much shorter. I will say a little more about this later; for now we need simply note the result, which is to allow the preceding New Kingdom (conventionally *c* 1550–1070 BC) to be lowered wholesale by some 250 years (see table opposite). As a consequence,

> Similar reductions could then be made in the chronology for the Late Bronze Age of the entire Mediterranean. As a result, the troublesome dark periods that infest the Iron Age cultures of the Old World would be shortened or, in some cases, eliminated (*CD*, p 261).

Unlike Rohl's books, *CD* does not focus on OT historicity. Only one chapter (40 of its 434 pages) is devoted to OT issues. Nevertheless, that chapter leaves no doubt that its proposals would have drastic implications for biblical archaeology. We will come back to this point later.

Should We Mind the Gaps?

The publication of *CD* sparked off a lively debate in archaeological journals. Establishment hackles were understandably raised by the thought that James and his fellow 'time bandits' had made off with two and a half centuries of ancient history.[12] Some objections will be mentioned below, but here it is worth dealing with a criticism that is often made of the authors' method.

In common with several other critics, Egyptologist Ken Kitchen alleged that James *et al* were making too much of ancient history's 'dark ages.' He charged them with collectively suffering from 'a constant paranoia about "gaps" and "dark ages" (which apparently have no right to exist).' Such gaps, according to Kitchen, 'are often simply gaps in modern knowledge, not in antiquity; they simply draw attention to what is yet to be discovered.'[13]

This sounds reasonable, but it misses the whole point of the argument, which is that the 'gaps' in question coincide across a wide geographical area and array of cultures. It seems unlikely that so many similar *lacunae* all result from accidents of preservation or discovery. In fact several examples come from the most heavily excavated parts of the world. Kitchen's comment trivializes problems that archaeologists in other fields find all too real. The 'gaps' highlighted by James *et al* cry out for something more than *ad hoc* explanations.

Another Egyptologist, James Hoffmeier, grasped this and commented:

> ...The authors have drawn attention to serious problems that cannot
> be ignored. Even if this study does not provide satisfying solutions to
> every case, the issues underscored should prompt the reassessment
> of all areas of Near Eastern chronology...[14]

Back to Basics

Could the conventional chronology be seriously wrong? To borrow a question from Job 38, 'On what were its bases sunk, or who laid its cornerstone...?'

The currently accepted chronology has not been handed down unchanged from the distant past, nor was it discovered by modern historians as an intact whole. It was pieced together bit by bit, through the hard work of scholars in many disciplines. What most scholars now take for granted as the framework of ancient history was not firmed up until the start of the 20th century. But just how firm is it? Could it have been distorted by an academic blunder made over a hundred years ago?

From the 7th century BC onwards, links between Egypt, Babylonia, Persia and Greece provide a secure chronology in which many events can be dated to within a single year. In terms of OT history, there is no doubt that Jerusalem was destroyed by Nebuchadnezzar in either 587 or 586 BC, or that Cyrus of Persia conquered Babylonia in 539 BC. The overlapping histories of Babylon and Assyria enable us to work back from this secure base to the start of the Neo-Assyrian period (c 900–612 BC). The Assyrian practice of keeping 'eponym lists' (in which each year was given the name of a different official) means that Assyrian chronology is accurate, to within a year, as far back as 911 BC.

This accurate chronology of the Neo-Assyrian period has proved useful for tying down OT dates for the period of the monarchy. The OT refers to five Assyrian kings, and Assyrian texts mention no less than eight kings of Israel and Judah. These connections enable us to use Neo-Assyrian dates to interpret and refine the chronological data in the books of Kings. The result is a chronology of the monarchy back to Solomon which is accurate to within less than a decade.

The end of the Neo-Assyrian period and the rise of the Neo-Babylonian empire were contemporary with the 26th Dynasty in Egypt, two of whose pharaohs are also mentioned in the OT. Pharaoh Neco (Necho II, 610–595 BC) killed Josiah when the latter tried to prevent him aiding Assyria against Babylon in 610 or 609 BC (2 Kings 23.29; 2 Chron 35.20–24); he then placed

Jehoiakim on the throne to rule Judah as Egypt's vassal (2 Kings 23.33–35). Neco was defeated by Nebuchadnezzar at the battle of Carchemish in 605 BC (Jer 46.2). Pharaoh Hophra (Apries, 589–570 BC) invaded Palestine during Nebuchadnezzar's siege of Jerusalem, but gave the city only a brief respite (Jer 37.5–8; 44.30).

These interlocking histories enable us to place the start of Egypt's 26th Dynasty at 664 BC, a fixed point shared by all parties in the chronology debate. It is as we work back from this date that uncertainties and disagreements begin to emerge.

Egyptologists borrow their framework for Egyptian history from Manetho, an Egyptian priest of the 3rd century BC. Manetho's original work has not survived, but from summaries preserved by other ancient writers we know that he divided Egypt's history (from King Menes, first unifier of the land, to the Persian reconquest of Egypt in the 4th century BC) into thirty dynasties. Modern Egyptologists have adopted his sequence, dividing it up as follows:[15]

Archaic Period (Dynasties 1–2)	3000–2700 BC
Old Kingdom (Dynasties 3–8)	2700–2136 BC
First Intermediate Period (Dynasties 9–10)	2136–2023 BC
Middle Kingdom (Dynasties 11–12)	1986–1795 BC
Second Intermediate Period (Dynasties 13–17)	1795–1540 BC
New Kingdom (Dynasties 18–20)	1540–1070 BC
Third Intermediate Period (Dynasties 21–25)	1070–664 BC
Late Period (Dynasties 26–30)	664–332 BC

Manetho recorded the reign-lengths of a good many pharaohs, but this information is not always preserved. Even when it is, the surviving summaries often disagree over the figures. Since the decipherment of Egyptian hieroglyphs in 1822, contemporary inscriptions have enabled Egyptologists to confirm or amend much of this data and to put flesh on its dry bones.

The TIP of an Iceberg

Moving back in time from the 26th Dynasty we come to the Third Intermediate Period (TIP for short), consisting of Dynasties 21–25. The length of the TIP is at the heart of the chronology debate. It is clear that its dynasties were not strictly concurrent. At times they overlapped, exercising limited rule from different centres. It is the extent of the overlapping that is questioned by the revisionists.

The length of the TIP is a complex topic and the reader will be spared the details. But it is important to remember what is at stake. Any adjustment to the length of the TIP will affect not only Egypt, but the whole of the ancient Near East, because so many neighbouring cultures rely on links with Egypt for their dates. As James *et al* put it:

> What has not been fully appreciated is that *for every doubtful year of Egyptian history granted to the Third Intermediate Period, another year is added to the Dark Ages of the Eastern and Central Mediterranean, the Near East and Africa.* (CD, p 232, emphasis original)

Hence any *shortening* of the TIP also *shortens* the chronologies of these neighbouring regions.

James *et al* and Rohl have pointed to similar evidence for shortening the TIP (*CD*, pp 234–238, 242–245; *TT*, pp 43–107). They agree that the start of the 21st Dynasty should be redated from *c* 1070 BC to *c* 840 BC. Beyond this, they part company.

Rohl also 'folds' the preceding 20th Dynasty, and overlaps most of this with the TIP as well. This allows him to reduce the dates of earlier New Kingdom pharaohs by almost an extra century, producing his reduction of nearly 350 years. James and his colleagues find problems with this (some of which we noted in Chapter 3), and regard a reduction of 250 years as 'an absolute maximum (and possible optimum).'[16]

After following the debate closely for some years, I agree with this conclusion. The revision outlined in *CD* may lack Rohl's exciting correlations between Egypt and the OT, but it solves more problems, and raises fewer new ones, than Rohl's more drastic reduction.

There are objections to the *CD* revision which we do not have space to examine here. Personally I am convinced that none of them amount to immovable obstacles.[17] But even if the *CD* model eventually turns out to be unworkable, that would not automatically mean a return to the *status quo*. There are other proposals on the table that would also have implications for biblical historians and archaeologists if they turned out to be correct.

Graham Hagens has argued that the TIP should be shortened by about 75 years, with a consequent reduction of New Kingdom dates by the same amount.[18] Aidan Dodson recommends a reduction of about 50 years, also made possible by shortening the TIP.[19] Dodson's conclusion is worth quoting:

> It is now apparent to a growing number of scholars that the chronological *status quo* is no longer an option; far less clear is any incipient consensus as to what precisely will replace it!

Shishak and Shoshenq— A Case of Mistaken Identity?

5

We now turn to an alleged link between Egypt and the OT—a link that, if sound, confirms the conventional chronology.

1 Kings 14.25–26 reports that 'in the fifth year of King Rehoboam, King Shishak of Egypt came up against Jerusalem; he took away the treasures of the house of the LORD and the treasures of the king's house; he took everything.' 2 Chronicles 12.1–9 also reports Shishak's invasion of Judah and adds various details.

The biblical Shishak is conventionally identified with Shoshenq I, founder of the 21st dynasty. The names Shishak and Shoshenq are undeniably a close fit. The 'n' is sometimes omitted from the Egyptian *Sh-sh-(n)q*, bringing it even closer to the Hebrew spelling. But names, however similar, are not enough to establish identity, and the conventional case also rests on the fact that Shishak and Shoshenq I both campaigned in Palestine.

Shoshenq I left an inscription at Karnak listing the towns he subjugated, and many of them are known from the OT and other sources. They are scattered over several regions: the coastal plain, the Jezreel Valley, part of Transjordan, the area of the Beth-Horon pass and parts of the Negev. His Palestinian campaign was evidently extensive.

An Immovable Rock?

The identification of Shoshenq I with biblical Shishak has become a linchpin of the conventional chronology. Thus Kitchen, reviewing *CD*, says: 'This is irremoveable, and on that rock alone, a 250-year shift is totally excluded.'[20] Is this so?

In fact, the identification of the two campaigns is not straightforward

In fact, the identification of the two campaigns is not straightforward. Central Judah is not represented in Shoshenq's list, and this is where Rehoboam's fortified cities were mostly situated according to 2 Chronicles 11.5–12. The Chronicler lists fifteen places that Rehoboam fortified, and clearly has these in mind when reporting that Shishak 'took the fortified cities of Judah' (2 Chronicles 12.4). Yet, of these fifteen, Shoshenq's list includes only one, Aijalon, on Judah's northwestern border.

Furthermore, Jerusalem itself is not mentioned in Shoshenq's list. This is particularly puzzling if the inscription is a record of Shishak's campaign. As a state capital that surrendered its independence (2 Chronicles 12.8), it should certainly have been listed. (A town did not have to be destroyed to qualify for inclusion, as some writers assume.)

Note also that, while the brunt of Shoshenq I's campaign seems to have been focused on the northern kingdom, biblical references to Shishak do not mention any foray into Israel. In fact 1 Kings 11.40 depicts Shishak as an ally, not an enemy, of Israel's king Jeroboam.

Kitchen has recently suggested that Jerusalem may have featured in a part of the list that is now damaged. However, he had previously (and convincingly) argued that the order of names in the list makes it 'unlikely' that Jerusalem was included in the damaged section, and he has not explained his change of mind.[21]

The admission that the two campaigns were not the same seriously weakens the identification

Another Egyptologist, Aidan Dodson, accepts that Jerusalem's absence from Shoshenq's list is a real problem for the conventional view. But he retains the identification of Shoshenq I with Shishak by suggesting that the campaign against Jerusalem could have occurred earlier in Shoshenq's reign than the one recorded at Karnak.[22]

This admission that the two campaigns were not the same seriously weakens the identification of the two kings. If there is no real match between the geo-political situations of the two campaigns, then the identity of Shishak and Shoshenq is open to question.[23]

A Circular Argument?

But what of the fact that the conventional chronology places Shoshenq I in the 10th century BC, alongside the biblical Shishak? The revisionists argue that it would amount to a circular argument to view this as proof of identity. In their view, the mass of evidence from the TIP's inscriptions has been arranged to fill a predetermined time-span, with the Shishak = Shoshenq equation playing an important role in determining that arrangement.

Kitchen, one of the chief architects of the conventional TIP chronology, objects that this is not the case, and that he constructed his chronology by 'dead-reckoning' back from the fixed date of 664 BC. 'On this basis, the absolutely exact correlation between Shoshenq I of the 22nd Dynasty and the Shishak who troubled Solomon's successor Rehoboam fits perfectly.'[24]

However, we may doubt whether the correlation was arrived at in a direct and utterly objective way. The identification of Shoshenq with biblical Shishak has been accepted by Egyptologists ever since Champollion proposed it in 1829. It quickly became a linchpin that kept Egyptian and OT chronologies in step through various adjustments to both, and was surely a premise that shaped Kitchen's reconstruction of the TIP.[25]

If Not Shoshenq, Then Who?

James *et al* redate Shoshenq I to the late 9th century BC. They suggest his campaign was directed not against Israel and Judah as such, but against an Aramean occupation, and that he may be identified as the anonymous deliverer who 'rescued Israel from the power of Aram' according to 2 Kings 13.5 (CD, p 385, n 134; also Rohl *TT*, pp 376–77).

With Shoshenq I redated to the late 9th century BC, who was the biblical Shishak?

With Shoshenq I redated to the late 9th century BC, who was the biblical Shishak who invaded Judah?

We have already seen that Rohl identifies Shishak as Ramesses II. He suggests that the biblical name Shishak is based on the Egyptian 'Sysw,' an attested abbreviation of Ramesses II's name. However, the difficulties we have noted for Rohl's overall scheme would rule out this identification.

James *et al*, with their less drastic shortening of Egyptian chronology, would identify Shishak as Ramesses III, whose name was sometimes abbreviated to 'Sessi'—another version of Ramesses II's 'Sysw' (CD, pp 203, 257, 385–86). This identification has gained attractiveness with a recent paper by Robert Drews, who suggests that Ramesses III conducted an offensive campaign into the Palestinian hill-country.[26]

6

New Alignments
in Biblical Archaeology

Although James and his colleagues devote only one chapter of CD to the implications of their revision for biblical archaeology, it is clear that those implications are far-reaching.

Here I will sketch some of them briefly and offer some assessment.

The archaeological period known as the Late Bronze Age is chronologically tied to Egypt. For example, scarabs and other items bearing the names of New Kingdom pharaohs turn up in Palestine's archaeological strata; imported pottery—for example Mycenean ware from Greece—occurs both in Egypt (in contexts that can be dated to the reigns of New Kingdom pharaohs) and in Palestine. These correlations mean that there cannot be any redating of Egypt's New Kingdom without an equivalent redating of the Late Bronze Age (LBA) in Palestine.

In terms of the *CD* revision, this means that the end of the LBA, currently dated between 1200 and 1170 BC, is redated to between 950 and 920 BC.

Lower dates for the LBA necessarily have a knock-on effect on the Iron Age which directly follows it. Conventionally viewed, the Iron Age lasted six centuries, ending with the Babylonian exile. Its subdivisions are dated (in round figures) as follows:[27]

Iron Age IA	1200–1150 BC
Iron Age IB	1150–1000 BC
Iron Age IIA	1000– 900 BC
Iron Age IIB	900–700 BC
Iron Age IIC	700–586 BC

Up Anchors!

Before outlining how a revised chronology would apply to the Iron Age, we must remove a potential misunderstanding. Many students of OT history and archaeology may be under the impression that certain Iron Age strata (occupation levels) are anchored firmly to the time of the Israelite monarchy.

For example, gates belonging to Iron Age IIA levels at Megiddo, Gezer and Hazor are regularly attributed to Solomon; Iron Age IIB levels at Samaria are attributed to Omri and Ahab; the last Iron Age IIC level at Lachish, containing the famous Lachish Letters, is assigned to the eve of the Babylonian exile.

These associations have become so much part and parcel of the conventional view that it is difficult to think in any other terms. The important thing to grasp is that none of these 'anchors' is more than hypothetical.

There is, for example, no evidence directly linking Solomon's reign with the monumental gateways of Iron Age IIA. The fact that gates of similar plan existed at Megiddo, Gezer and Hazor—three cities that Solomon (re)built according to 1 Kings 9.15—seemed striking when the coincidence was first noticed in the 1960s. But since then, similar gates have turned up from a later time (at Lachish) and from outside Solomon's realm (at Ashdod). Therefore there is no reason to associate this type of gate with Solomon.

Since the conventional attributions are hypothetical, the various subdivisions of the Iron Age can be redated *relative to OT history*. Putting it another way, redating Iron Age IIA does *not* involve redating Solomon. Solomon can keep his usual place in the 10th century BC while Iron Age IIA strata move to a later century. And Solomon will acquire a new background as another archaeological period, previously dated earlier than his reign, moves down to the 10th century BC. Within limits, archaeological periods and OT history can be realigned like the two parts of a slide-rule.

So, staying with Solomon, what is the result of redating the end of the LBA by 250 years?

Solomon: A Late Bronze Age monarch?

Lowering the end of the LBA to 950 BC, or soon after, would place it in the latter half of Solomon's reign. This has clear advantages over the conventional scheme. Although Gezer, Megiddo and Hazor have those monumental gates referred to earlier, the cities of Iron Age IIA are completely lacking in signs of wealth or imported luxury. The last phase of the LBA (known as LB IIB) is in sharp contrast to this.

The treasury of the last LBA palace at Megiddo contained a large cache of carved ivories. These reflected the artistic tastes of a wide area, including Egypt in the south and the Hittite realm in the north (compare 1 Kgs 10.29). Traces of a late LBA building in Egyptian style have been found just north of the Old City of Jerusalem (compare 1 Kgs 9.24). The plan of Solomon's temple reflects an architectural tradition known from LBA levels at Hazor and elsewhere. The ten bronze four-wheeled trolleys that Solomon had made for the temple (described in 1 Kings 7.27–37) have close parallels from the end of the LBA (*CD*, pp 197–200).

In short, the LB IIB period furnishes Solomon with the kind of background the biblical account of his reign would lead us to expect.

Iron Age 1: Settlement or Secession?

But if the later LBA restores Solomon's missing cosmopolitan refinement, in other respects the redating may seem bizarre.

The following period (Iron Age IA) saw the dramatic decline, even collapse, of many cities, the proliferation of small villages in the central hill-country, and a much poorer material culture. These phenomena are usually seen as evidence for the arrival and/or settlement in Canaan of the early Israelites. Can it really make sense to place such changes at the end of Solomon's reign?

There is no evidence for a major influx of newcomers at the start of the Iron Age. The new hill-country settlements were probably a response to the economic decline of the cities, and it is not difficult to identify this transformation with the end of the united monarchy.

Solomon's later years saw both political and economic deterioration (for example 1 Kings 9.10–14; 11.14–25). The trend would have accelerated with the division of the kingdom, ensuing internecine strife, Shishak's invasion and Aramean pressure. The collapse of Solomon's trade network would have hastened the economic decline of cities, forcing people to adopt new life-styles and exploit new areas in order to survive.

Insofar as any outside influences can be detected at the start of the Iron Age, they appear to have come from northern Transjordan. In a revised context, they could reflect the arrival of refugees from Rezon's raiding parties (1 Kings 11.24).

Iron Age 2A: Solomon or Ahab?

As we move to the later Iron Age, things become a bit more complex. Unlike the LBA, the Iron Age cannot be redated wholesale by 250 years.

The *beginning* of the Iron Age naturally has to be redated by the same amount as the end of the LBA, but its *end* cannot be moved by the same amount of time (for reasons we cannot go into here). At the very most, the end of the Iron Age may be dated 150 years later than at present. So if its beginning is redated by 250 years, there will have to be some overall compression of the period if its length is to be reduced by about a century (that is, to *c* 500 years, *c* 950–*c* 450 BC). In fact there is a good deal of flexibility in the length of time assigned to the various subdivisions of the Iron Age, so some telescoping of the Iron Age as a whole is possible.

James *et al* redate the start of Iron Age IIA (conventionally containing Solomon's reign) to around 875 BC. In their view, buildings that have previously been attributed to Solomon should be understood as the work of Ahab (*c* 873–853 BC), an energetic builder according to 1 Kings 22.39.

At Samaria their redating resolves a number of problems. According to 1 Kings 16.23–24, the city of Samaria was founded half way through the reign of Ahab's father Omri (*c* 885–873 BC). Kathleen Kenyon, the British excavator of Samaria, therefore attributed the first phase of buildings to Omri. However, the pottery underlying the earliest buildings is conventionally dated to the 11th–10th centuries BC (Iron Age IB). Hence a recent assessment of Samaria's archaeology concluded that there had been 'a fairly long occupation prior to the time of Omri,'[28] in spite of the fact that 1 Kings 16.24 does not suggest this. With Iron Age IB redated to the early 9th century BC, Samaria's earliest pottery falls into place as the evidence of Omri's activity.

At Samaria, their redating resolves a number of problems

Kenyon attributed the second phase of Samaria's buildings to Ahab, in spite of the fact that Omri spent only a few years there. It is more logical, James *et al* suggest, to assume that Ahab continued to develop the first phase. They assign the second phase to Jeroboam II (*c* 793–753 BC). Most of Samaria's beautiful ivories are generally dated to this phase and hence, in Kenyon's scheme, to the time of Ahab (compare 1 Kings 22.39). In the *CD* model they would illustrate the luxurious 'houses of ivory' and 'beds inlaid with ivory' against which Amos protested (Amos 3.15; 6.4).

The Lachish Letters: Jeremiah or Nehemiah?

Later in Iron Age II Assyrian cultural influence reached Palestine, and this provides James *et al* with further criteria for lowering the traditional dates (*CD*, pp 180–183). One result is a redating of Strata III and II at the city of Lachish.

The end of Stratum III is currently linked with Sennacherib's campaign of 701 BC (see 2 Kgs 18.13-14), but in the *CD* model it is reassigned to Nebuchadnezzar's invasion, *c* 587 BC. The end of Stratum II is moved down in turn from *c* 587 BC to *c* 440 BC. This involves redating the famous Lachish Letters to the post-exilic period (*CD*, pp 171–175).

To readers familiar with the conventional scenario this may sound ludicrous. The Letters are usually thought to fit perfectly in the time of Jeremiah. However, James *et al* argue persuasively that the situations reflected in the letters correspond more closely with the time of Nehemiah. One example will have to suffice here.

They argue that the situations reflected in the letters correspond more closely with the time of Nehemiah

Letter III contains a reference to a 'letter of Tobiah, servant of the king' that was sent to one Shallum *via* 'the prophet'; the content of Tobiah's letter is summed up by the warning 'Beware!'

This recalls the situation in Nehemiah 6.10–19. Nehemiah's enemy here is Tobiah, governor of Ammon. Tobiah's title 'the servant' (Neh 2.10) is generally thought to be short for 'the servant of the king,' indicating high office. This Tobiah sent intimidating letters to Nehemiah (Neh 6.19) and also used prophets to do his dirty work (Neh 6.12–14). In short, this Tobiah has the same name, the same status, and did the same things as the Tobiah mentioned in Lachish Letter III.

A line in Letter IV is generally thought to confirm the conventional date of the Letters. This mentions the cities of Lachish and Azeqah in a context that suggests they faced a military threat. It therefore invites comparison with Jeremiah 34.7, which refers to the capture of Judean cities by the Babylonian army. Lachish and Azeqah are named there as 'the only fortified cities left in Judah' apart from Jerusalem. However, as James *et al* point out, 'As closely neighbouring cities, Lachish and Azeqah must have been endangered by common threats on many occasions' (CD, p 173).

It is not yet clear whether their late date for the last phase of the Iron Age can be sustained

In their view, the military crisis reflected in Letter IV was a Philistine incursion. This ended Lachish Stratum II around 440 BC (*CD*, p 175).

Although James *et al* have offered an attractive reinterpretation of the Lachish Letters, it is not yet clear whether their late date for the last phase of the Iron Age (Iron Age IIC) can be sustained. Other inscriptional evidence may turn out to prevent it.[29] But this would by no means vitiate the whole scheme. If Iron Age IIC has to end earlier than proposed in *CD*, the consequence would simply be a greater compression of the Iron Age II period as a whole. In fact some scholars are independently arguing for a shorter Iron Age II.

Recent Trends

Since the publication of CD, support for a reduction of Iron Age dates has come from various quarters.

A redating of Iron Age IIA–B strata seems to be demanded by the well-known 'House of David' inscription from Tel Dan. Fragments of this Aramean inscription, referring to the defeat of a 'king of the house of David,' were found reused as building stones. The most recent, detailed study of the inscription dates it shortly after 800 BC,[30] but its breakage and reuse as building material evidently occurred later than this. A reassessment of Tel Dan's stratigraphy suggests that its reuse happened in Stratum IVA, conventionally dated no later than the 10th–9th centuries BC. A reduction of dates has therefore been urged, not only for Stratum IVA at Tel Dan, but for all strata with the same pottery.[31]

Among Israeli archaeologists there is now a growing school of thought favouring lower (that is, later) dates for early Iron Age strata. Israel Finkelstein has argued for redating strata normally assigned to the 11th–9th centuries by almost a century.[32] In a recent study of Tel Arad's chronology, Ze'ev Herzog lowers the earliest Iron Age strata from the 12th–11th centuries BC to the 10th–9th centuries BC.[33] Although these archaeologists do not acknowledge any debt to previous scholarship, their reductions are of exactly the same order as those in the CD model, and they have the same effect of reassigning 'Solomonic' levels to the time of Ahab.

However, unlike the authors of CD, these Israeli scholars do not question the current chronology of Egypt. As a result, they work with the conventional date for the LBA/Iron Age transition (that is, c 1180 BC). Their lower dates for the Iron Age II period therefore produce a very drawn-out Iron Age I. This is proving controversial, not least because of its implications for the united monarchy.

A result of redating Iron Age II without also redating the end of the LBA is that Solomon is left with only scant Iron Age I remains to his name. This has added fuel to a heated debate over the historicity of the early monarchy, fostering the view (often labelled 'minimalist') that Solomon's reign was largely, if not wholly, fictional. This consequence is, of course, avoided if lower dates are adopted for Egypt's New Kingdom and Palestine's LBA strata.

This brings us back to one of the questions with which we began: Does the historicity of the OT matter?

7   Does It Really Matter?

The last three decades have seen a drastic diminution of confidence in the OT's historicity.

As we saw in chapter 2, the majority of scholars no longer believe there was an Exodus or a Conquest, and many doubt that the united monarchy was anything more than a small tribal kingdom. Some even doubt its existence.

David Rohl blames this scepticism on the apparent lack of correlation between the OT narratives on the one hand and ancient Near Eastern history and archaeology on the other. For him, the OT lacks confirmation from archaeology because 'an artificially extended chronology for the ancient world' has 'detached the historical narrative of the Bible from its true archaeological setting' (*Lost Testament*, p 3).

I believe there is some truth in this diagnosis (though the prevailing scepticism also has other, more complex, roots). However, I have tried to explain why I do not think Rohl's alternative is workable. His exciting new links between Egypt and the Bible are, unfortunately, illusory.

I have also tried to show why I do not favour a return to the *status quo*. In my view, the authors of *CD* have made a convincing case for shortening the chronology of the ancient Near East. It so happens that their alternative has considerable fall-out for biblical archaeology. But that is not my main reason for favouring it. It is because of its problem-solving power in so many other areas that I find it compelling and worth investigating.

Having said that, I do welcome the fact that it lends plausibility to certain biblical narratives.[34] This is because I agree with John Goldingay that, in many cases, 'The historical "having happened-ness" of the story matters.'[35]

History and Story

There has long been a move in literary studies of the OT to replace 'history' with 'story' as a category for understanding biblical narrative. In many respects this has been a good thing. By focussing attention on the text it has been a corrective to the older view which saw events in Israel's history, rather than the Bible itself, as the locus of revelation.

But for many scholars, 'story' is not merely *different* from history, but can actually be *divorced* from it. G W Ramsey comments:

> The telling of a story does not in and of itself constitute a claim that the events narrated actually happened. The story has a world of its own, whether based on actual events or not. *As a story* it is not dependent on its correspondence with actual historical realities.[36]

For some scholars, history is a completely inappropriate genre for understanding the OT narratives. T L Thompson finds it significant that there is no word for history in biblical Hebrew. He believes the Old Testament writers made a distinction between history—which they viewed as 'illusory'—and reality, which could only be evoked through story and metaphor.[37] N P Lemche welcomes the fact that 'the interpretation of the text of the Old Testament...has to a large extent been liberated from historical considerations,' and that the biblical narrative can at last be 'studied as what it is—a narrative.'[38]

There are several issues here, but they can be summed up in a single question: What kind of writings are the OT narratives? It is, I think, self-evident that the OT narratives are not history-writing in any modern, Western, sense. But it would be a mistake to deduce from this that the OT writers did not think in terms of history at all. J Maxwell Miller has argued:

> The biblical writers were very conscious of history, and the Bible itself may be looked upon as largely historical in format and content. It is not history written for the sake of history, of course, and not history of the sort one would read in a modern history book... Nevertheless, the theological messages that the biblical writers sought to convey are so thoroughly intermeshed with their perceptions of history that it is difficult to separate one from the other.[39]

From a different perspective, John Goldingay has emphasized that the stories in the Old Testament are not merely works of human imagination but a *witnessing* tradition.

> As witness, their stories have reference, not merely sense...If the stories lacked any historical reference they would arguably also lack sense; they would self-deconstruct. To seek to understand biblical stories in their own right leaves quite open the possibility that they need to have, and do have, some historical reference in order to 'work' as stories.[40]

Hence he finds the category of story important but insufficient as an approach to the OT narratives. He regards much OT narrative as more, not less, than history.

These insights are helpful when we ask how far historicity matters. Many OT narratives are written with a literary artistry that distinguishes them sharply from modern history-writing. Their authors were not trying to achieve an exact correspondence between the narrative and actual events. To think otherwise is to commit the fundamentalist fallacy. Rather, the OT narrators were interested in the significance of events, and they highlighted these creatively.

For example, there is little doubt that the writer of 1–2 Kings crafted the speech of the Assyrian commander in 2 Kings 18 to bring out the theological significance of Judah's confrontation with the super-power of the day (is trust to be placed in human resources or in Yahweh?). Goldingay agrees, but still credits the author with 'a deep concern for what actually happened, in that he seeks to trace the working out of the will and word of God precisely in what happened in Israel's history.'[41]

Of course not all parts of the OT share the need for historical reference. Issues of genre become important in deciding which these are, though this is not the only criterion. Personally, I consider Job and Jonah to be pieces of literary theology whose claim upon me does not depend on their 'having happened-ness.'[42]

Chronology and Historicity

Do we need a revised chronology to disclose or defend the historicity of the OT? There are certainly many books that do that with some success within the conventional chronology,[43] so perhaps the answer is 'no.'

But there is also the question of historical truth, which is surely worth knowing (if it can be known!) for its own sake. My own interest in the chronology debate is driven largely by this.

And there is another point, which makes the chronology debate relevant in a broader sense to anyone studying the OT. In spite of the fact that knowing dates has been out of fashion in the learning of history, chronology is important for the historian, biblical or otherwise. As the archaeologist Colin Renfrew noted in his Foreword to *CD*:

> Chronology is the backbone of archaeology as well as of history. For without a time framework there can be no established sequence of events, no clear picture of what happened in the past, no knowledge of which significant development came first.

From a biblical perspective one could add: there can be no clear socio-political history of the ancient Near East against which to understand the origin of Israel, its rise to statehood, or its exile and restoration.

We should not need, or expect, historical confirmation of OT narratives in order to take them seriously as texts that can reveal God and nurture faith. But neither should we be surprised if many turn out to be historical. Personally, I would be more surprised if they turned out not to be!

Notes

1   These are Rohl's new dates for Ramesses II, as given in *Lost Testament*, p 454; the dates proposed in *TT* were 11 years later.
2   I Finkelstein, online at: http://www.bib-arch.org/bswbBreakingIllSpecial1a.html
3   The entire interview is online at: http://tlc.discovery.com/convergence/eden/expertqa.html
4   See the online interview in note 3 for Rohl's clearest statement of his personal beliefs.
5   For criticisms by a conservative scholar see B G Wood, 'David Rohl's Revised Egyptian Chronology: A View from Palestine,' *Near East Archaeological Society Bulletin* 45, 2000, pp 41–47, online at www.christiananswers.net/abr/scoop.html where it is occasionally updated. W R Mattfeld, who rejects OT historicity, critiques Rohl at www.bibleorigins.net/RohlsChronologyDeconstructed.html The most comprehensive critique is C Bennett, 'Temporal Fugues,' *Journal of Ancient and Medieval Studies* 13 (1996), pp 4–32; accessible online at www.christiananswers.net/abr/docs/temporalfugues.rtf
6   For information visit http://groups.yahoo.com/group/NewChronology. Some articles from *JACF* can be found online at http://www.nunki.net/PerRenput/Reaction/index.html
7   J J Bimson, *Redating the Exodus and Conquest* (JSOT Supplement 5), (Sheffield, 1978, 2nd edition 1981).
8   In *The Lost Testament* Rohl raises the date for the end of the Late Bronze Age to *c* 886 BC (p 452). However, this conflicts with other parts of his revision and so does not solve the Samaria problem. For details see accompanying online resources on the Grove website http://www.grovebooks.co.uk
9   For a detailed discussion of this point see Bennett, as in note 5 above.
10   Colin Renfrew in the Foreword to Peter James *et al*, *Centuries of Darkness* (see following note) p xv.
11   Peter James, I J Thorpe, Nikos Kokkinos, Robert Morkot and John Frankish, *Centuries of Darkness: A challenge to the conventional chronology of Old World archaeology* (London: Jonathan Cape, 1991).
12   For a list of over 90 reviews, and quotations from over 30, both favourable and unfavourable, see the *Centuries of Darkness* website: www.centuries.co.uk
13   K A Kitchen, 'Blind Dating,' *Times Literary Supplement*, May 17, 1991, p 21; Kitchen made similar criticisms in 'Egyptian Chronology: Problem or Solution?' *Cambridge Archaeological Journal* 1/2, 1991, pp 235–239. For responses see James *et al*, 'Centuries of Darkness: A Reply to Critics,' *CAJ* 2/1, 1992, pp 127–130. Their debate with Kitchen also ran for four issues of the *Times Literary Supplement*.
14   J K Hoffmeier, review of *CD* in *Biblical Archaeology Review* 19/6, Nov–Dec 1993, pp 6–10.
15   The dates are taken from K A Kitchen, 'Regnal and Genealogical Data of Ancient Egypt (Absolute Chronology I): The Historical Chronology of Ancient Egypt, A Current Assessment,' in *The Synchronization of Civilizations in the Eastern Mediterranean in the Second Millennium BC*, M Bietak (ed) (Vienna, 2000) pp 39–52.
16   P J James, N Kokkinos and I J Thorpe, 'Mediterranean Chronology in Crisis,' in *Sardinian and Aegean Chronology*, M S Balmuth and R H Tykot (eds), (Oxford: Oxbow Books, 1998) p 34. For more detail see the Grove website at http://www.grovebooks.co.uk
17   For a survey of some objections see the Grove website.
18   G Hagens, 'A critical review of dead-reckoning from the 21st Dynasty,' *Journal of the American*

Research Center in Egypt 33, 1996, pp 153–163.

19 A Dodson, 'Towards a minimum chronology of the New Kingdom and Third Intermediate Period,' *The Bulletin of the Egyptological Seminar* 14, 2000, pp 7–18.

20 K A Kitchen, 'Centuries of Darkness,' *Times Literary Supplement*, Letters, June 21, 1991.

21 See originally K A Kitchen, *The Third Intermediate Period in Egypt (1100–650 BC)* (Warminster: Aris and Phillips, 1973, 2nd edition 1986, reprinted with new material 1996) p 298; for his latest view see 'The Shoshenqs of Egypt and Palestine,' *Journal for the Study of the Old Testament* 93, 2001, p 11.

22 A Dodson, 'Towards a Minimum Chronology of the New Kingdom and Third Intermediate Period,' *Bulletin of the Egyptological Seminar* 14, 2000, p 8.

23 I have dealt with this more fully in 'Shoshenk and Shishak: A Case of Mistaken Identity?' *Journal of the Ancient Chronology Forum* 6, 1992/93, pp 19–32. See also I Finkelstein, 'The Campaign of Shoshenq I to Palestine,' *Zeitschrift des Deutschen Palästina-Vereins* 118, 2002, pp 109–135 (whose alternative conclusion I do not agree with, however).

24 Kitchen, 'Egyptian Chronology: Problem or Solution?,' *Cambridge Archaeological Journal* 1/2, 1991, pp 235–36; more recently, 'The Shoshenqs of Egypt and Palestine,' *JSOT* 93, 2001, pp 5–6.

25 For example the correlation between Shoshenq I and Shishak depends in part on reign-lengths achieved by a creative distribution of anonymous year-dates; see P J James and R Morkot, 'Centuries of Darkness,' *Times Literary Supplement*, June 7, 1991, p 15, and P J James, 'Centuries of Darkness,' *TLS*, July 12, 1991, p 13.

26 R Drews, 'Medinet Habu: Oxcarts, Ships and Migration Theories,' *Journal of Near Eastern Studies* 59, 2000, pp 161–190.

27 Following E Stern (ed), *New Encyclopedia of Archaeological Excavations in the Holy Land* (London: Simon and Schuster, 1993) vol 4, p 1529.

28 R E Tappy, *The Archaeology of Israelite Samaria*, Vol 1 (Atlanta, 1992) p 67.

29 A study of this question is currently being conducted by one of my PhD students, Peter Van der Veen.

30 G Athas, *The Tel Dan Inscription: A Reappraisal and a New Interpretation* (Sheffield: Sheffield Academic Press, 2003).

31 R L Chapman III, 'The Dan Stele and the Chronology of Levantine Iron Age Stratigraphy,' *Bulletin of the Anglo-Israel Archaeological Society* 13, 1993/94, pp 23–29. Athas (*The Tel Dan Inscription*, p 5) fails to appreciate the force of Chapman's argument.

32 I Finkelstein, 'The Archaeology of the United Monarchy: an Alternative View,' *Levant* XXVII, 1996, pp 177–187.

33 Z Herzog, 'The Fortress Mound at Tel Arad: An Interim Report,' *Tel Aviv* 29, 2002, pp 3–109.

34 In addition to the fitting background it provides for Solomon, the CD scheme also offers an improved context for my identification of the Conquest with the end of the Middle Bronze Age (outlined in Chapter 2). The authors briefly refer to this (CD, p 368), although they do not deal specifically with the issue.

35 J Goldingay, 'How Far Do Readers Make Sense? Interpreting Biblical Narrative,' *Themelios* 18/2, 1993, pp 5–10.

36 G W Ramsey, *The Quest for the Historical Israel: Reconstructing Israel's Early History* (London: SCM, 1981) p 123, emphasis original.

37 T L Thompson, 'Historiography of Ancient Palestine and Early Jewish Historiography: W G Dever and the Not So New Biblical Archaeology,' in *The Origins of the Ancient Israelite States*, V Fritz and P R Davies (eds) (Sheffield: Sheffield Academic Press, 1996) p 41.

38 N P Lemche, 'Early Israel Revisited,' *Currents in Research: Biblical Studies* 4, 1996, p 9.

39 J M Miller, 'Reading the Bible Historically: The Historian's Approach,' in *To Each Its Own Meaning: an introduction to biblical criticisms and their application*, S McKenzie and S Haynes (eds) (London: Chapman, 1993) p 14.

40 J Goldingay, *Models for Interpretation of Scripture* (Carlisle: Paternoster, 1995) p 32.

41 J Goldingay, '"That You May Know That Yahweh is God"—A Study in the Relationship Between Theology and Historical Truth in the Old Testament,' *Tyndale Bulletin* 23, 1972, p 85.

42 I have dealt in more detail with the issues in this section in 'Old Testament History and Sociology,' in *Interpreting the Old Testament: A Guide for Exegesis*, C Broyles (ed) (Grand Rapids: Baker, 2001) pp 125–155.

43 For example K A Kitchen, *The Bible in its World: The Bible and Archaeology Today* (Exeter: Paternoster, 1977); J D Currid, *Ancient Egypt and the Old Testament* (Grand Rapids: Baker, 1997); J K Hoffmeier, *Israel in Egypt: The Evidence for the Authenticity of the Exodus Tradition* (Oxford: OUP, 1997). Kitchen's major work on this topic, *On the Reliability of the Old Testament* (Grand Rapids: Eerdmans, 2003) was still awaited at time of going to press.